Curriculum Visions

The Stone Age

A stone circle

Using a Stone Age 'dibber'

A CVP Book © Earthscape 2008

Author
Brian Knapp, BSc, PhD

Editor
Gillian Gatehouse

Senior Designer
Adele Humphries, BA, PGCE

Designed and produced by
EARTHSCAPE

Printed in China by
WKT Company Ltd

The Stone Age – Curriculum Visions
A CIP record for this book is available from the British Library

Paperback ISBN 978 1 86214 571 9

Illustrations
All illustrations by *Mark Stacey* except the following: *David Woodroffe* 27tr.

Picture credits
All photographs are from the Earthscape Picture Library except the following (c=centre t=top b=bottom l=left r=right): *Alamy* 36–37; *NOAA* 7; *ShutterStock* 1 (main), 2 (main), 3 (inset), 16, 20–21, 24–25 (main), 26–27, 28–29, 30–31; *Sigurd Towrie/www.orkneyjar.com* 34–35 (main); *Wikipedia Creative Commons* 6, 31, 35 (inset).

This product is manufactured from sustainable managed forests. For every tree cut down at least one more is planted.

In this book we shall use the word Britain as a shorthand to mean the British Isles. The break up of the British Isles into its various countries is too recent to have any meaning during Stone Age times.

Contents

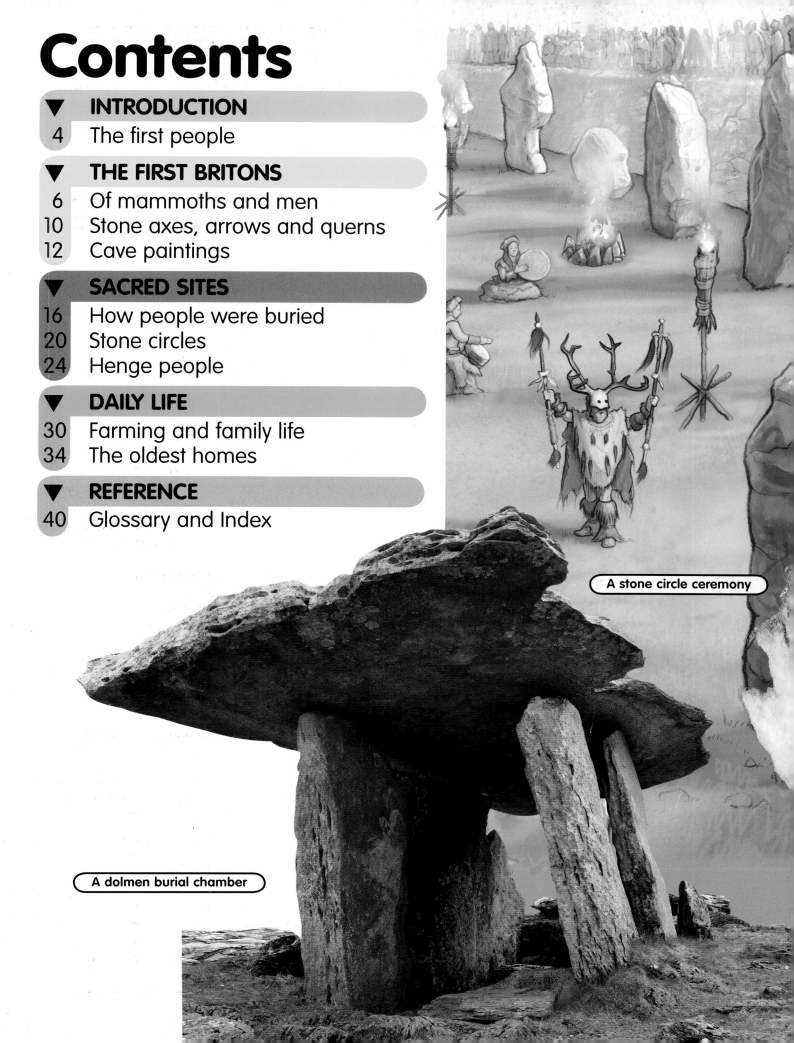

A stone circle ceremony

A dolmen burial chamber

The first people

This book is about the very ancient British, the ancestors of most of us who live in Britain even today. It is a book about a long lost time called the Stone Age. Only fragments from that time remain, but they hint at a most extraordinary history.

Here is a summary of what happened in Britain up to the end of **STONE AGE** times, that is between 700,000 years ago and about 2200 years BC, or 4,200 years ago.

1 The earliest humans that we know of lived in Africa over 4 million years ago. There were not many of them and they only spread to other places slowly because they had no particular reason for moving.

2 This is why the first people to arrive in Britain did so only 700,000 years ago (picture ①). We know them as 'Upright Man'. They made the first flint hand axes (page 11) and also fashioned things from animal bones and wood.

3 Between the times when ice spread over most of Britain, other people began to live here. Between about 300,000 years and 30,000 years ago they were **NEANDERTAL** people. They were similar to us, but not directly related. About 200,000 years ago, our direct **ANCESTORS** 'Wise Man' (*Homo Sapiens*) started to move out of Africa. By about 30,000 years ago they were painting in the caves of Europe, but they did not get as far as Britain. At this time the Neandertals became **EXTINCT**.

4 About 12,000 years ago the ice melted away again. The people who came back to our land were our direct ancestors.

▶ ① **When the first people explored Britain as the Ice Age was ending, this is what Wales and Scotland might have been like.**

5 For a while after the **Ice Age**, the sea level was much lower than it is now and Britain was connected to the rest of Europe by land. In fact, people hunted in what is now the North Sea because, until the sea level rose, it was home to many wild animals.

6 Once the sea level rose Britain became a group of islands.

7 Being a group of islands didn't stop trade, it didn't stop the **British** from doing things independently or from learning new ideas from the continent. From about 6,000 years ago people learned how to farm and began to settle down. From 5,000 years ago people built giant structures, including Stonehenge.

8 By about 4,200 years ago (2,200 BC), people had learned how to make bronze metal and later they learned how to make iron. Gradually they gave up using stone for making tools. As a result, the Stone Age came to an end. But there was no great break in traditions, and just as we continue to build cathedrals out of stone today, so the people continued to build their religious monuments out of stone long after the end of the Stone Age.

years ago	STONE AGE TIMELINE
4 million	The first humans
1.8 million	Humans reach Europe
700,000–200,000	Early people live in Britain during warm periods within the Ice Age, and leave evidence of stone hand axes
200,000–60,000	Ice Age prevents anyone from living in Britain
40,000–30,000	Neandertals lived in Britain, making hand axes and other flint tools. By 30,000 years ago they had become extinct. Our ancestors had also arrived and their remains are found in the burial caves of Paviland in South Wales and Kent's cavern, Devon.
20,000–15,000	Ice Age prevents anyone from living in Britain
15,000	The ice sheet begins to melt away
14,000	The first modern humans (*Homo Sapiens*) arrive in Britain to eat the plants and wild animals that have returned after the cold of the Ice Age. People are buried in Gough's cave, Somerset. They trade stone axes with other groups hundreds of kilometres away. It was still cool and few trees grew. The people lived on wild horse, reindeer and other wild animals. They had no permanent dwellings and lived in simple tents.
10,000	End of the Old Stone Age, or Palaeolithic
10,000–6,000	Mesolithic period, or Middle Stone Age, during which time Britain became a group of islands
6,500	The rising sea level cuts the British Isles off from mainland Europe. The climate becomes warmer and forests start to grow. New animals now live in these forests, such as roe deer, wild pig and wild cattle and they are hard to hunt. Dogs become tamed and are used for herding. People settle across the whole of the British Isles as far as Orkney and Shetland. Crops are grown and animals herded for the first time. There are now enough people in Britain to make it impossible to wander about hunting animals. People organised into groups and claimed areas as their territory. They began to make polished stone axes and to make pottery. People clear woodland by fire and replace it with crops. Trade with mainland Europe brings new ideas and probably some people from mainland Europe also arrive.
6,000	The New Stone Age, or Neolithic period begins
5,800	People begin to make stone houses in Orkney (and probably elsewhere) and to build burial mounds (long barrows) and construct stone circles. Changes to the environment are seen as people put wooden causeways over bogs in Somerset. The Celtic language might have been introduced into Britain about this time as a result of trading with people on the mainland of Europe.
4,900	People make the famous ditched monuments, or henges, such as Stonehenge. Wooden bowls are used and bows made.
4,200	People discover (probably through trade) how to make the metal copper and then, a few hundred years later, how to make the much harder metal bronze. The Stone Age time ends and the Bronze Age begins, and metal weapons replace flint axes. Nevertheless, many techniques of the Stone Age carry on into the Bronze Age and, for example, the last part of building Stonehenge happened in the Bronze Age.

Of mammoths and men

The first people to walk in Britain arrived three quarters of a million years ago and found a land where woolly mammoths and rhino roamed.

This is the story of one of the most remarkable events in the world. It is about how Britain got its people and ways of life. This book is about finding out how our ancestors came to be here, what they did and what they thought.

The Ice Age and before

The first creatures that we call human-like, lived in East Africa about 4 million years ago. Their search for food caused them gradually to wander into new lands, and by 2 million years ago there were human-like people (called Upright Man) in Europe. But this was also the time of the last Ice Age, when, from time to time, the world became colder and ice sheets spread south from the poles. The ice flowed across the countryside, gouged out deep valleys in the mountains and spread what it had scraped away as great thicknesses of bouldery clay all over the lowlands, at least as far south as London and Cornwall. Each time the ice advanced, it wiped the slate clean of any trace of human living.

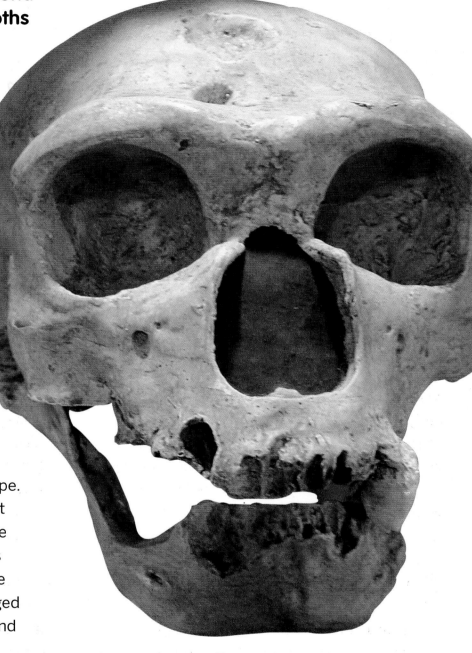

▲ ① **The skull of Neandertal man.**

The first footsteps in Britain

There were three or four times when ice spread down to cover most of Britain. During each part of the Ice Age the sea level fell so

THE FIRST BRITONS

▶ ② **Skulls of modern man (Wise Man – *Homo Sapiens*)**

much that the British Isles were not islands, but part of Europe. For a while after the ice melted away, the sea level did not rise and early people and animals could have walked from what is now Spain or Denmark to Dublin or the Shetlands without getting their feet wet.

About 700,000 years ago the first people whose remains have survived arrived in Britain. They made stone tools to cut up the hide and meat of woolly mammoths (picture ③ on pages 8–9), horses, deer and many other animals.

It would have been hard work killing a mammoth with stone tools. A group of people would probably have needed to chase it for days until the animal was exhausted. Then they could finish it off with stone axes and spears.

Some time later, these 'Upright men' were forced out of Britain by the advance of ice.

Then, when the ice melted, another group of human-like people arrived. These were called Neandertal people (picture ①). But, although for almost three quarters of a million years, Upright Man and Neandertal Man lived in Britain, they were not our direct ancestors. Our real ancestors were still in Africa. About 200,000 years ago, this branch of humans (called 'Wise Men', *Homo Sapiens*, picture ②), our ancestors, arrived and lived alongside Neandertal people in Europe. Then about 30,000 years ago the Neandertals became extinct. Some people think that our ancestors might have killed them, but it is unlikely we will ever know for sure. In any case, when the ice finally retreated 15,000 years ago, it was only our real ancestors that came back because the Neandertals were dead.

Weblink: www.CurriculumVisions.com

▼ ③ The woolly mammoth was a creature of cold conditions (just as polar bears are today), but it would have been a challenge for early people to hunt and kill it because they did not have efficient weapons.

Stone axes, arrows and querns

The Stone Age people used knives, axes and querns – all made from stone.

How did people make the stone tools they used, and where did the idea come from?

If you go to a place where hard, brittle rocks are common, such as the chalk hills of England, you will find flints lying about. They are mostly fist-sized pieces of very hard rock (called nodules), but some have naturally broken and show sharp edges. This, surely, is where early Stone Age people got the idea of making axes.

You can use an untouched flint nodule to bash things (picture ①). It could be used to soften meat by beating it, for example, but you can't cut with it. For that you need to get a very sharp edge. So it must have been that one day someone was knocking these nodules together and a piece flaked off one of them. Such flakes have an edge as sharp as a modern knife (picture ③).

The flake could be broken down and shaped into an arrowhead, using another stone or even a bone or a twig, and it could be put in a split branch and used as a spear.

The main part of the flint, called the core, could also be shaped by knocking off flake after flake until the core would fit comfortably into the hand. As a result the hand axe was developed (picture ②). It lasted as the main tool for hundreds of thousands of years.

Towards the end of Stone Age times people began to grind off the flints and so make the surface smooth (picture ④).

Clothes made of skins

Flint core being worked on

Fragments of flint scattered on the ground

▲▶ ① Natural flints are chunky and only useful for crushing.

▲ ② The earliest hand axes (this one is about 400,000 years old) were roughly knapped.

▶ ③ Thin flakes were used as knives and scrapers.

Knocking pieces off a flint is called **KNAPPING**. You sit down and put a piece of hide on your upper leg as protection, then place a nodule on your leg and give it a sharp glancing blow with another nodule. Eventually, and with a lot of skill, you will get good flakes coming off and you will start to make a hand axe. Wherever you sit, you would leave a lot of small useless pieces behind. So, wherever we find such remains we know that many people sat there knapping, possibly hundreds of thousands of years ago.

QUERNS are pairs of grindstones (see picture on page 31) and are also made of stone, but a completely different kind of stone. Two stones are rubbed together to crush grains of wheat, barley and so on. For this you need rough stones, not flint. Sandstones and basalt rocks were often chosen. Here the task was to make one stone rounded (and you might well be able to pick one of those from the river) and rub a saddle-shaped dip in a larger stone. Then you placed a handful of grains in the saddle and rubbed with the round stone. It was slow work, but effective – just like most of Stone Age living.

▼ ④ By the end of the Stone Age, hand axes were being smoothed and polished and given a proper edge.

Flint nodules

Flint used for knapping

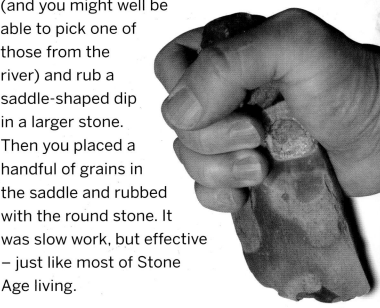

Cave paintings

Stone Age people thought of dark caves as special places. Here they painted the animals they hunted, perhaps for similar reasons that people made stained glass thousands of years later.

Being able to draw and paint is a rare skill. But even when you have no written language, you can show in paintings what your life was like and what was important to you (picture ①).

The earliest known European cave paintings that have so far been discovered were probably made by our direct ancestors about 30,000 years ago (picture ②). They show deer, bison and even rhinos. These paintings were made in Spain and France during the last part of the Ice Age, when no one could live in Britain.

Although there is no way of knowing exactly why people made these cave paintings, we know they must have taken considerable skill and effort, so they would have been important things to do. The people did not live in the caves, so they must have been places of special importance, perhaps early kinds of temple that were visited by people whenever they were in the area.

They tell us that the people were very skilled, and that they worked together and chose to do things that were not just a matter of survival. They may have drawn on cliffs and other exposed rocks out in the open as well as in the dark reaches of caves,

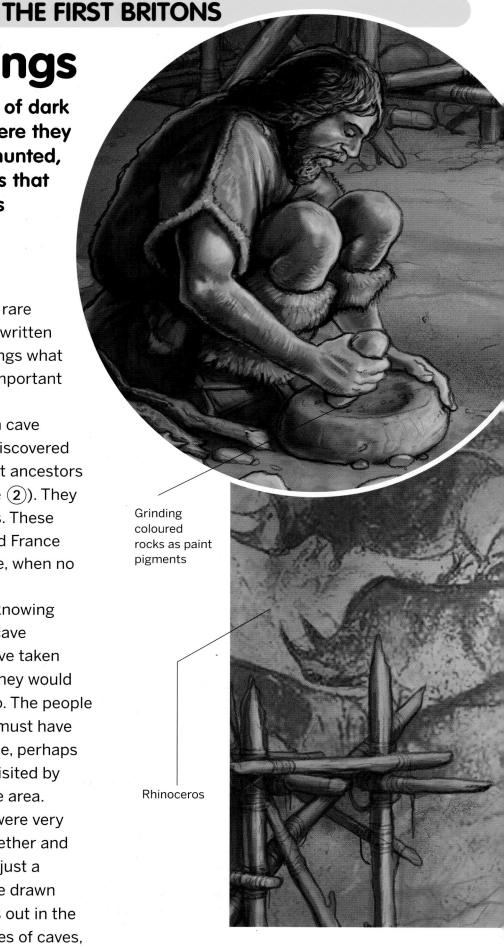

Grinding coloured rocks as paint pigments

Rhinoceros

but the drawings and paintings exposed to the weather have long since been lost. But a remarkable 350 caves still have paintings.

The paintings must have been made using the light from burning branches. They were never seen as we see them today with our powerful artificial lights.

◄▼ ① **A reconstruction of cave painting about 30,000 years ago.**

They used charcoal or the soot from a fire (carbon) to make the **PIGMENT** (colour) for black, and they crushed coloured stones to make red and yellow. Then they mixed these pigments with natural plant and animal gums, and painted with their fingers, or, for more delicate work, used feathers, bunches of animal hairs, quills and sticks as brushes.

Burning branch for light

Grey limestone wall of cave

Burning fat for light

Crushed end of stick for painting

Frame for painting at high level

Grinding and mixing pigments

14

▼ ② This scene is a reconstruction of what the Chauvet cave in France might have been like at the time of the wall paintings. The art shows hunting animals, such as bear, as well as grazing animals, such as bison and rhinos.

How people were buried

Many people were cremated, but some were buried in tombs called long barrows.

For many tens or even hundreds of thousands of years, Stone Age peoples have respected their dead.

Cave burials

The oldest known burial in Europe was found in the Gower region of South Wales (the Paviland cave) by the Reverend Buckland in 1823. He called the skeleton that he found the 'Red Lady of Paviland' (although it later turned out to be a man aged about 21). We can read about the actual find:

"[I found the skeleton covered] by a coating of a kind of [red dye] ... which stained the ... surface of the bones ... Close to ... where the pocket is usually worn ... [were] about two handfuls of [periwinkle shells]. [Next to] the ribs [were] forty or fifty fragments of ivory rods [also] some small... rings ....".

We now know the skeleton is 26,000 years old, making it the oldest modern human remains ever found here. The body may have had the flesh removed before it was laid out, the head removed and the bones then stained with red. People had taken a lot of time and trouble. The rings and ivory rods show that he had been buried with things that were precious to people at the time (they are called grave goods).

Passage graves

This skeleton was preserved because it was in a cave, but bones buried in open

▲ ① **A simple dolmen.**

fields would rarely have survived. So it is not until people buried their dead in stone coffins that we find their remains again. A single stone coffin is called a **DOLMEN**. It has a slab of rock for a roof and some upright stones to hold the roof in place. The body was placed under the slab and the whole thing covered with soil to make a mound. These were first made about 6,000 years ago (4,000 BC). The biggest, however, have a long passage leading to a central chamber where the bones were placed. They are called passage graves. The best known of these are La Hougue Bie in Jersey and Newgrange in Ireland. La Hougue Bie is the smaller, with a 20 m long stone-covered passage leading to the central chamber. The tomb was buried by 12 m of soil! The Newgrange passage grave is immense and is also special because swirling decoration was etched in the giant standing stones and passageways, and then painted.

Long barrows

Passage graves are circular. Long barrows are shaped like modern coffins. You can see these long, thin burial chambers high up on the chalk hills at Wayland's Smithy and West Kennet in Oxfordshire, for example. Wayland's Smithy is 60 m long and 13 m wide at the end with the giant standing stones (picture ② below, and ③ on pages 18–19). It was built between 5,700 years ago and 5,400 years ago (that is hundreds of years before the time of Stonehenge).

A stone passage leads to a cross-shaped burial chamber close to one end. Giant standing stones were placed where the passage begins. Smaller 'kerb stones' were placed upright around the edge of the tomb.

When it was examined, the bones of 22 people were found. These may have been the last of many people laid to rest there. The burial chambers and passage were covered with chalk and soil from nearby ditches.

▼▶ ② **The giant stones and gallery (below) and the burial chambers at the end of the gallery (right) as they appear today. On the next page is a reconstruction of what it might have been like when the barrow was in use.**

The passage, or gallery, faces south, so the early morning sun would shine along it at midsummer. (At Newgrange it is the midwinter sun that shines along the passage.)

None of these things could have been built without large groups of people working together. But when would they do this, as most of them moved about following the animals they hunted? They must all have arranged to meet at special times of the year, and what easier time to work out, when you don't have a watch, than midsummer or midwinter?

These barrows were more than just places to bury the dead. It is possible that the people believed that although bodies decayed, the spirit of the dead survived and that it needed a 'home'. Many people around the world have believed this, and some do today. A spirit home could be a house, or it could be an area of ground set aside for the spirits. In a way, this is how many people still see modern religious buildings and cemeteries, too,

So the long barrow may have been a place reserved for spirits.

Imagine the scene. After a massive effort the people would have cleared an area of forest and made a space where the barrow would be built. Then they put up giant standing stones. These stones separated the world of the living from the world of the dead. They made the chambered graves from more stones and then heaped chalk and soil over them, creating two long ditches beside the barrow. Then they finished off the edges with smaller kerbstones. Then the stones may have been

Entrance passage or gallery

Painted designs on rocks

Priest with deer skin and antlers

World of the living

Members of the clan of the buried person

painted brightly using swirling and zig-zag patterns (just as the temples of ancient Egypt were painted, and our churches used to be painted).

Between the standing stones was a passage, or gallery, down which the priests may have crawled carrying the remains (perhaps just the bones) of a body. As the priest went along the passage, he went behind the giant standing stones and so carried the dead into the spirit world. Probably, no one else was allowed on the land behind the stones; that was only for the spirits. Everyone else gathered in front of them.

Then, at the end of the ceremony, a large stone may have been rolled across the passage, sealing it until another ritual burial needed to be held.

The barrows ceased to be used 5,000 years ago. Any paint faded, the natural colour of the stones returned and what really happened was lost in the mists of time. But if you visit these sites, they still hold an almost magical sense of mystery.

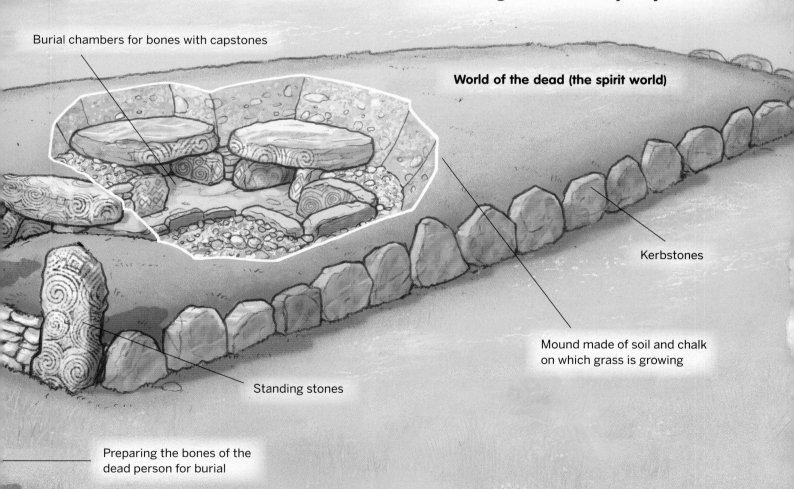

Burial chambers for bones with capstones

World of the dead (the spirit world)

Kerbstones

Standing stones

Mound made of soil and chalk on which grass is growing

Preparing the bones of the dead person for burial

▲ ③ This is a reconstruction of what a burial might have been like at a long barrow. We do not know exactly what ceremonies were like.

Stone circles

Over 5,000 years ago people made some of the most remarkable features the world has ever seen. They are the circles of massive standing stones.

When people say Stone Age, most of us think first of the great stone circles like Stonehenge. But that is only a part of the picture. Welcome, again, to the Neolithic spirit world.

It is important to know that the stone circles were NOT the first things to be built in Stone Age times. Indeed, the mightiest stones of all – those at Stonehenge – were put up after the end of the Stone Age (that is, in the **BRONZE AGE**). This is why we have looked at burials first, because the burial barrows are older. As we said with the barrows, they were more than just places to bury people, they were probably where people gathered, and a place on Earth where the spirits of the dead could live. A spirit home could be a house, or it could be an area of ground set aside for the spirits, like the area of the barrow. Or it could be marked out by standing stones placed in a circle. It was all a matter of what was fashionable at the time. Here we are going to look at stone circles. This does not include Stonehenge, even though you might think it is the best example of a stone circle. That is because Stonehenge is a henge, not just a stone circle and so we will look at it on pages 25–27.

▲▼ ① Castlerigg in summer and in winter.

Stone circles are almost unique to the British Isles. This suggests that, by this time, with Britain no longer being connected to Europe by land, the ancient British were developing ideas of their own.

We have to realise that we have absolutely no real idea why these stones were put up. To many modern people they look like a giant clock, which is why many people have tried to find connections between the stones and midsummer's day or midwinter's day.

It is useful to remember, too, that as we move through Stone Age times, there are more people and so it is likely that much bigger events were staged than in the times before.

It is also likely that ideas changed, so while the long barrow (pages 17–19) was the spirit world for a small number of people, there was now need to find a place for a larger number of spirits, or a more respectful way to worship them. For this reason the standing stones in front of the barrow may have been developed into a circle of standing stones (and, by the way, many standing stones were at first standing timber posts and only later replaced with stones).

There are many, many stone circles (there are 18 in Dartmoor National Park alone), mostly about 25 m across. The most famous are, however, far bigger. Avebury (also a henge, page 25) is 400 m across.

So the smaller circles may have been local worship sites ('churches') and places like Avebury may have been places to which people from far and wide came on seasonal pilgrimages ('cathedrals'). If the inside of the circle was now the spirit home of the dead, it is likely only the priests were allowed in here and everyone else stayed outside the circle.

Whether small or large, these stone circles, like the barrows before them, needed the backbreaking toil of lots of people. The biggest giant stones (called megaliths) may have needed the efforts of thousands of people at a time, first to drag the stones to where they were to be put up, and then to dig pits and get the stones upright (remember that a slab of stone will topple over in soft soil unless it is placed with about half its height in the soil).

Castlerigg

The oldest surviving stone circle in Britain is Castlerigg, near Keswick in Cumbria (picture ① on pages 20–21, and ② below). It was built 5,200 years ago. It is made of forty stones of local rock placed upright in the soil. The weightiest is about 16 tonnes. It is roughly 30 m across. Inside it is a smaller rectangular space marked out by more stones, and also some burial pits.

There is a gap in the northern part of the circle, which may have been an entrance.

▼ ② **Castlerigg at sunset.**

▼ ① Some of the giant Outer Circle stones at Avebury henge.

Henge people

A henge is a circle made of a bank and a ditch. To begin with they often had rings of wooden posts, then standing stones inside them. They are by far the biggest structures of Stone Age times.

Have you ever wondered how Stonehenge got its name? It is a 'HENGE' where the *stone* slabs are the most striking feature (picture ②, and ③, ④ and ⑤ on pages 26–27). So what is a henge? It is a circular ditch and bank made by people in the Stone Age. Henges may have, or had, stone slabs or wooden posts inside them, but the stone/wood circles are often less old than the ditches and banks.

If you were part of a small, independent clan, you would have no use for a stone or wood circle, or a henge. So we can also tell that by 5,000 years ago, our ancestors made up a connected society who were prepared to come together and regularly work, and perhaps worship, at a common place. As we find henges from Scotland to southern England, we can guess that all of Britain shared some common beliefs.

It is not clear why henges with stone circles in them were built in some places but just henges or stone circles in others.

▲ ② **Stonehenge on midsummer's day. (Note that the sun rose in a slightly different position when the henge was in use.)**

However, a henge takes at least as much effort to make as putting up standing stones (except perhaps in the case of Stonehenge), so a henge was really important. It had to be built where there were lots of helpers.

There are many henges, and although Stonehenge has the biggest standing stones, it is not the biggest henge. That is at Avebury, which is a massive 400 m across (picture ①, and ⑥ on pages 28–29).

When it was finished 4,800 years ago, the henge ditch at Avebury was 13 m deep and the bank made from the material in the ditch was 9 m tall. At first it looks like a fort, with the bank designed to keep people out, but the ditch and bank are the wrong way round for that. Instead it must simply be to separate out two parts of the landscape. Inside the ring may have been a 'sanctuary', the home for the spirit world or where gods were worshipped. You see examples of sanctuaries in both ancient Egypt and in ancient Greece. At Avebury, there are also 96 standing stones in the Outer Circle.

Henges developed over a long period of time and ideas may have changed. Indeed, some people think there were stone circles which had a henge built around them, and some people think there were henges that had stone circles built within them. Certainly the posts and stones of many henges were rearranged several times.

Stonehenge

Stonehenge is one of the most famous prehistoric sites in the world. In fact, the word 'henge' may come from an older word meaning gallows (medieval gallows had two uprights and a cross piece, like the **TRILITHONS** of Stonehenge).

Its ditch and bank were probably dug about 5,100 years ago and the whole site given a face-lift several times, finishing with the giant trilithons which were added about 4,100 years ago (which is in Bronze Age time – *after* the end of the Stone Age). Notice that this is an enormous timespan. It is thought that maybe people even first put up three standing posts 6,500 years ago when the land was still wooded and before farming had begun.

The Stonehenge that we see today began when a circular bank and ditch 110 metres across was dug. By this time the surrounding land was farmed and the area was open grassland. The ditch was dug in sections, almost as though many groups of people were each made responsible for their own part of the ditch. Inside the ditch may have been a ring of standing timbers (see picture ⑤, top).

▲ ③ A trilithon (tri means '3'; lith means 'stone' – two uprights and a horizontal).

▼ ④ Stonehenge trilithons, looking across the henge ditch.

More standing timbers were put up about a century later. At this time the bank was made lower and the ditch partly filled in. At this time, too, the site was also used as a burial ground and many cremations took place. This makes it the earliest cremation cemetery in the British Isles.

About 4,600 years ago two sets of holes were dug and 80 standing stones, each 2 m high and 1 m wide and weighing 4 tonnes, were placed in them. A single large stone (now called the Altar Stone) was also placed at this time.

The north eastern entrance was widened to match the direction of the (then) midsummer sunrise and midwinter sunset. Four stones, known as Station Stones were also placed here, two of which are on mounds (known as barrows, but which do not contain burials). The Avenue, a pair of ditches and banks stretching 3 kilometres to the River Avon, was also dug at this time.

About 4,400 years ago 30 giant stones were brought from a nearby quarry and set up in a 33 metre circle with a ring of 30 lintel stones resting on top (see picture ⑤, bottom). Each standing stone was around 4 metres high, 2 metres wide and weighed around 25 tonnes. These were the first stones to be worked into shape, rather than being natural shapes. For example, the lintel stones curve slightly to continue the circular appearance of the earlier monument. However, the circle, if it was meant to be a

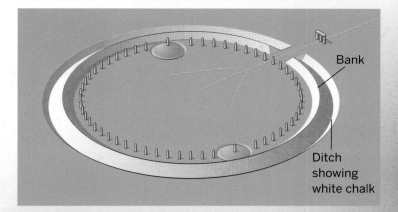

Bank

Ditch showing white chalk

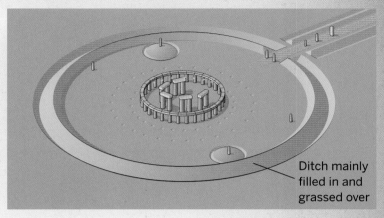

Ditch mainly filled in and grassed over

▲ ⑤ **These diagrams show what Stonehenge may have looked like when it was first built (top) and at a much later stage (bottom). Notice that the ditch has partly been filled in and grassed over and that many stones have been added and some removed.**

circle, was never completed (it would have needed 74 stones). Finally, inside this circle, five trilithons (each of 2 uprights and 1 lintel, the biggest stones of all) were placed in a horseshoe-shape 14 metres across with its open end facing the entrance to the henge. The uprights weigh 50 tonnes.

All of this was finished by 4,100 years ago. Although many of the stones were moved at a later date, Stonehenge continued to be used until Iron Age times and the arrival of the Romans.

Bank

Ditch

▼ ⑥ This is a reconstruction of what a ceremony at Avebury Henge might have been like.

Inner circle of standing stones

Priests performing ceremonies

Ceremony being watched by crowds of people who have all gathered at Avebury for the celebration.

Bank made of white chalk rubble dug from the ditch

Ditch

Outer circle of standing stones

Entrance to the henge

Farming and family life

Towards the end of the Stone Age, people were able to make comfortable lives for themselves. They had also already began farming.

As we have seen, the earliest Stone Age people ate berries and nuts, hunted animals and moved with the wild herds. They would have cut them up with sharpened stone tools (pages 10–11).

Because plants can only be harvested for a short part of the year, people were probably forced to rely on meat for most of their food. They did not understand how to crush cereal grains and they had no domesticated animals, so they did not eat bread of any kind, nor drink milk or eat any kind of dairy produce. But they did eat some leaves and roots.

Almost farming

It was easier to move with a herd of deer that was munching its way over the land, than to go charging after big game. Deer bunch up into a herd when threatened and so are easier to catch. The Lapps of northern Europe still do this kind of what is called 'loose herding' today.

Because these were wild animals our ancestors were on the move, so they might well have lived in portable tents made of tree branches covered in hides, like the Lapps and other people still do.

This is important, because it means that most Stone Age people didn't need any kind of permanent building. So we find their stone tools, but nothing else.

Then about 23,000 years ago, ideas of farming spread from the Middle East, across Europe to Britain. People found out how to crush cereals between grindstones (querns) (picture ②).

As the Neolithic period (the last part of the Stone Age) arrived, real farming began (picture ① below, and ③ on pages 32–33).

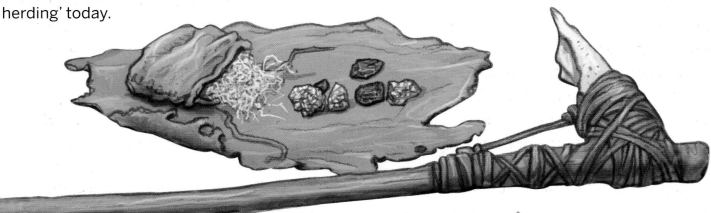

◀▼ ① **Stone Age bark bag, firelighting materials and hoe.**

▲ ② **A Stone Age quern consisting of a round rubbing stone and a dished saddle stone.**

Interestingly, the Neolithic period was also the first time that people experienced the famines that have haunted every period of history since. This is because they were now settled, planted seed, and depended on harvests. When the harvests were good they did well, but when they failed, they went hungry. Before (when there were fewer people) they were able to keep on hunting.

During the Neolithic period fishing became a common way of getting extra food for the first time. People also started to domesticate cattle, sheep, goats and dogs. Ploughing was introduced, and little fields began to be formed in what had previously been continuous woodland. Perhaps they made their fields by burning the trees, picking the worst of the boulders from the topsoil and planting seed in the tree ashes.

Settling down had good and bad points. It meant more food could be got from the land (unless harvests failed) to feed the increasing numbers of people. But it also meant that people started to pollute the rivers for the first time, and disease became more common.

What did later Stone Age people wear? Weaving was unknown, except at the very end of Stone Age times, when people wove grass and flax stems to make into cloaks. Most people wore clothes made from animal skins held together with bone pins. Wool and the kind of clothing we know today would have to wait until the Bronze Age (and you can read about this in the Curriculum Visions book 'Celtic times').

Patch of forest land cleared by burning to make a farmstead

▼ ③ This is a reconstruction of what Neolithic farming might have been like. The stones in the fields are left over from Ice Age times.

Stock pens

Simple communal building

Close herding

Baskets

Chopped and partly burned tree trunks from the cleared forest

Until ploughs were introduced from Europe people used this combination of stone and wood 'chop down and pull' hoe.

The whole family were involved in farming

Birch bark bag containing flint and other material to make a fire.

Animal skin clothing with tendon string and bone pins

A dibber for planting seeds

Leather sandals

Hoe

The oldest homes

Britain has the oldest homes in northern Europe. They show how sophisticated life was in Orkney five thousand years ago.

As people settled down, they tended to build permanent shelters. In many parts of the country these were made from tree trunks and branches.

▼ ① **The Stone Age village of Skara Brae, Orkney.**

As these have long rotted away we have no real idea what they were like. But in some places, such as the Orkney Islands of northern Scotland where wood was not easily available, people built the first stone houses in Europe (pictures ①, ②, ③ on pages 36–37, and ④ on pages 38–39).

▼ ② The farmhouse at the Knap of Howar, Papa Westray.

Knap of Howar and Skara Brae

At the Knap of Howar on Papa Westray island, there is a Neolithic farmhouse that may well be the first stone house ever. It was built about 5,500 years ago and people lived in it for 400 years. This farmhouse is a pair of rooms joined by a low passageway (picture ②).

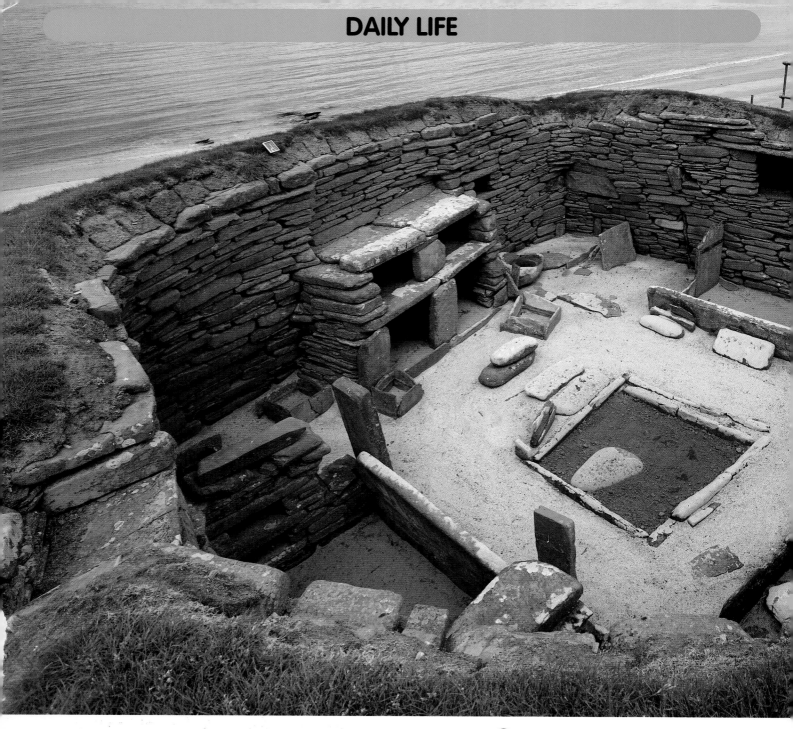

▲ ③ The interior of one of the Neolithic Orkney houses.

A few hundred years later, a village was built at nearby Skara Brae (picture ① on pages 34–35, ③ above, and ④ on pages 38–39). Ten houses have been uncovered so far, although there is evidence that more remain buried. They are joined together by underground passageways. They were built and lived in between about 5,100 and 4,500 years ago (about the same time as the earliest part of Stonehenge was being built). Then, for a reason we do not know, they were abandoned and sand covered them up, preserving them until they were excavated quite recently.

What you now see are the stone walls (1.6 m high) and passageways connecting the houses (picture ① on pages 34–35).

whale bones, was laid, making a conical roof which was thatched with turf or even seaweed gathered from the nearby beaches. All of the roof material has long since rotted away.

Each house measures about 40 square metres, and consists of a large square room with a large hearth for heating and cooking.

The people probably made some furniture out of wood, but they also made several stone-built pieces of furniture, including what we now think are beds, cupboards, seats and storage boxes. The most prominent item in each room is something that looks like a dresser. As you entered the room it was straight ahead. It may well have been a place where the remains of ancestors were kept and treasured, but no-one can be sure.

The houses even had soakaway toilets and drainage channels inside the rooms.

In the nearby rubbish tips (**MIDDENS**), archaeologists have found pieces of cattle, sheep and pig bone, so we know these early farmers reared animals. There are also barley and wheat grains, so they must have cultivated the nearby land (which means it must have been warmer and drier than it is now). They caught the kind of fish that cannot be caught from the shore, but would have had to be caught using boats. They also used clay pottery.

So it turns out that, five thousand years ago, at the time when the early ancient Egyptians were building their pyramids, Orkney folk (Orcadians) were very sophisticated, too, sitting warm and comfortable in nice little weatherproof stone houses.

The nearby rocks readily break up into slabs, making it easy to use them as bricks. Nevertheless, they were expertly fashioned so they fit together. This dry-stone walling is not entirely windproof, which is why the houses were partly dug into the ground, thereby using the soil as insulation.

It is likely that on the tops of these walls a frame of roof timbers, or even

▼ ④ This is a reconstruction of what life at Skara Brae might have been like.

The Atlantic ocean with its winter gales and storms

Roof supports of driftwood, whalebones, etc.

'Dresser' (possibly a place for ancestor remains)

Shelf

Bed

Hearth

Quern

38

The lower parts of the walls were buried in soil and domestic waste to help keep out the wind

Low level passageways hidden from strong winds

Glossary

ANCESTORS People from whom we are descended and who lived a long time ago.

BRITISH, BRITONS People who lived in the lands we now call the British Isles. It is used in this book as a general shorthand for the native peoples of the islands.

BRONZE AGE The time between 2200 BC and 800 BC when the main metal for making tools was bronze. The Bronze Age followed the Stone Age.

DOLMEN A simple grave made of three upright stones with a capstone on top acting as a lid. The stones were buried under a mound of soil.

EXTINCT A group of living things who are no longer alive because every member of the group has died.

HENGE A circular ditch dug to mark out the boundary of a religious site.

ICE AGE During the last 2 million years, there have been several long, cold spells when ice sheets formed and spread over many parts of the world including Britain, making much of the land uninhabitable. The whole period is called the Ice Age. But Ice Age times have not been all cold. In-between the coldest, ice-sheet times there have been much warmer spells when the ice melted away.

KNAPPING Shaping stones by skilfully striking one against another using a glancing blow.

MIDDEN An ancient rubbish tip that has been preserved. Middens provide rich sources of material to help us understand what ancient times were like.

NEANDERTAL MAN (also spelled Neanderthal) and named after where the first specimen was found, in the Neander Tal (Neander Valley) in Germany. They were human-type people who lived between 300,000 and 30,000 years ago. They were not our direct ancestors.

PIGMENT The material used to make colour in a paint. In Stone Age times it was crushed rock or charcoal.

QUERN A pair of stones used for grinding cereal grains to make flour.

STONE AGE The time when tools were mainly made out of stone. In Britain, the Stone Age ended about 2200 BC, that is 4,200 years ago.

TRILITHON A group of three (tri) standing stones (lithon), two upright and one horizontal lintel stone, joining the uprights to make a kind of doorway.

Index